MW00365047

Circle the sentence.

1. The dog is barking.   Fuzzy the cat.

Circle the word that is spelled correctly.

2. bok   book   buk   bouk

Make two words in the -*an* family.

3. _____ an   _____ an

Write your first and last name.

4. _____

Finish the sentences.

1. The _____ squeaks.

2. The _____ purrs.

3. The _____ barks.

dog

mouse

cat

Fix the sentence.

4. i ride the bus

_____

WEEK 1 Wednesday

Fix the sentence.

1. my dad lives in new york

_____

Could it be true?

2. The hen walked on the road.   yes   no

3. The pen walked on the road.   yes   no

4. The men walked on the road.   yes   no

WEEK 1 Thursday

Choose the best word. Write it on the line.

1. Mr. Black is tall. _____ can reach the top. (Him   He)

2. Dr. Smith is short. _____ can't reach the top. (She   Her)

Circle the words that rhyme with _bell_.

3. shell   yellow   well   tell

Fix the sentence.

4. i go to the dance last saturday

_____

WEEK 1 — Friday

Write the words in the group where they belong.

Things with Wheels	Things with Legs
_____	_____
_____	_____
_____	_____
_____	_____

Word Box

car   dog   van   bike   cat   man   wagon   boy

WEEK 1 — My Progress

How many did you get correct each day? Color the squares.

	Monday	Tuesday	Wednesday	Thursday	Friday
4					
3					
2					
1					

WEEK 2 Monday

Fix the sentence.

1. the ball is big and round

_____

Write the word that means more than one.

2. ball _____

3. dog _____

4. boy _____

WEEK 2 Tuesday

Make two words in the -ill family.

1. _____ ill _____ ill

Fix the sentence.

2. mary is first in line

_____

Could it be true?

3. The mouse ate the cheese.　　　yes　　no

4. The house ate the cheese.　　　yes　　no

WEEK 2 Wednesday

Circle the word that is spelled correctly.

1. da   dae   day   dai

Write the two words for each contraction.

2. didn't _____ and _____

3. it's _____ and _____

Fix the sentence.

4. will you come too

_____

WEEK 2 Thursday

Fix the sentence.

1. she gave me a bok

_____

Choose the best word. Write it on the line.

2. The girls _____ the ball.   (kick   kicks)

3. Sammy _____ the cake.   (eat   eats)

What happens next?

4. Milton gets in the car.

   He goes to the store.   **OR**   He brushes his teeth.

WEEK 2 — Friday

Sue's birthday party will be on October 1 at 3 o'clock at the skating rink. Help her fill out the invitation.

Come to my party!

Date: _____

Time: _____

Place: _____

Sue

WEEK 2 — My Progress

How many did you get correct each day? Color the squares.

	Monday	Tuesday	Wednesday	Thursday	Friday
4					
3					
2					
1					

WEEK 3 Monday

Circle the words that rhyme.

1. ball   bug   fall

2. mitt   man   pan

Fix the sentence.

3. what a big dog

_____

Write the numeral.

4. two _____   four _____

WEEK 3 Tuesday

Write whose it is.

1. It is the _____ kite.

2. It is the _____ hat.

Choose the best word. Write it on the line.

3. I _____ a wasp in the bus.   (saw   seen)

Fix the sentence.

4. the teacher read to us

_____

WEEK 3 Wednesday

What happened next?

1. The wind blew, so...

   the flag waved. **OR** the train whistled.

2. The light turned red, so...

   the cat meowed. **OR** the truck stopped.

Make two words in the *-all* family.

3. _____all   _____all

Fix the sentence.

4. my birthda is in august

_____

WEEK 3 Thursday

Circle the words that mean more than one.

1. cat   dogs   boy   girl   cars

Write the names in ABC order.

2. Max   Betty   David

   _____   _____   _____

3. Sam   Tonya   Rick

   _____   _____   _____

Fix the sentence.

4. we will sing with mrs black

_____

WEEK 3 Friday

Read the story.

Paul looked out the window.
He saw the street.
Two boys went by.
They had a bat and a ball.

Continue the story. Write what you think the boys will do.

_____

_____

_____

WEEK 3 My Progress

How many did you get correct each day? Color the squares.

	Monday	Tuesday	Wednesday	Thursday	Friday
4					
3					
2					
1					

WEEK 4 Monday

Circle the words that make a sentence.

1. She gave me a book.   To the first grade.
2. Little Red Riding Hood and the wolf.   The teacher read to us.

Circle the word that is spelled correctly.

3. game   gaim   gam   gamm

Fix the sentence.

4. gia will win the race

_____

WEEK 4 Tuesday

Answer the questions.

1. Can a bird have a nest?   yes   no

2. Can a bird have a house?   yes   no

3. Can a bird have a truck?   yes   no

Fix the sentence.

4. who came to your party

_____

WEEK 4 **Wednesday**

Write the opposite.

1. down   _____

2. little   _____

big
up

Circle the word that is spelled correctly.

3. werk   wirk   work   wrk

Fix the sentence.

4. tony and maria lik to play ball

_____

Daily Language Review

WEEK 4 **Thursday**

Use *me* or *I* to finish the sentences.

1. _____ can read a book.

2. Sam gave the box to _____ .

3. My dad and _____ like to fish.

Fix the sentence.

4. i live in denver

_____

WEEK 4 Friday

Number the pictures in order. Then write about what happened.

_____

_____

_____

_____

WEEK 4 My Progress

How many did you get correct each day? Color the squares.

	Monday	Tuesday	Wednesday	Thursday	Friday
4					
3					
2					
1					

WEEK 5 **Monday**

Make two words in the *-at* family.

1. _____ at   _____ at

Find the names. Fix the letters that should be capitals.

2. ryan   boy

3. girl   rosa

Fix the sentence.

4. can you read the buk

_____

WEEK 5 **Tuesday**

Circle the words that rhyme with *dog*.

1. log   dig   hog   frog

Answer the questions.

2. Can a fish use a CD player?   yes   no

3. Can a cat take a nap?   yes   no

Fix the sentence.

4. peter has a red hat

_____

WEEK 5 Wednesday

Circle the word that is spelled correctly.

1. kume   come   cume   cahm

Choose the best word. Write it on the line.

2. _____ went to the park.
        We   Us

3. Dad made _____ popcorn.
                we   us

Fix the sentence.

4. i go to scott elementary school

_____

WEEK 5 Thursday

Circle the word that does _not_ belong.

1. dog   cat   bird   mouse

2. grass   tree   rock   flower

3. star   house   sun   moon

Fix the sentence.

4. sam and bill went to see zack

_____

WEEK 5 Friday

Unscramble and write the words to make a sentence.

1. Hernaldo   fish.   fed   the

   _____

2. swimming.   go   Let's

   _____

3. lunch.   my   I   have

   _____

4. Please   with   me.   come

   _____

WEEK 5 My Progress

How many did you get correct each day? Color the squares.

	Monday	Tuesday	Wednesday	Thursday	Friday
4					
3					
2					
1					

Circle the words that mean more than one.

1. lions   monkey   tigers   elephant

Write the two words for each contraction.

2. can't _____ and _____

3. don't _____ and _____

Fix the sentence.

4. did he open the door

_____

Make two words in the -ish family.

1. _____ish   _____ish

Circle real or make-believe.

2. Polly made a picture.   real   make-believe

3. Pat lives on the moon.   real   make-believe

Fix the sentence.

4. dad will kum to the party

_____

WEEK 6 Wednesday

Circle the word that is spelled correctly.

1. with   witt   weeth   wiht

Choose the best word. Write it on the line.

2. She _____ like to run.
       don't   doesn't

3. We _____ going home.
       was   were

Fix the sentence.

4. trudy can't go wth us

_____

WEEK 6 Thursday

What might happen next?

1. Gina plants a seed.
   The seed sprouts. **OR** Gina pets the cat.

2. The dog barks.
   Tom feeds the cat. **OR** Tom lets him in.

Read the sentence. Then answer the question.

3. Andy only likes cuddly animals.
   Would Andy like snails?   yes   no

Fix the sentence.

4. john hit the ball

_____

WEEK 6 Friday

Write the word that tells about each animal.

_____   _____   _____

| big | bigger | biggest |

WEEK 6 My Progress

How many did you get correct each day? Color the squares.

	Monday	Tuesday	Wednesday	Thursday	Friday
4					
3					
2					
1					

WEEK 7 Monday

Make two words in the *-ed* family.

1. _____ed   _____ed

Read the sentence. Then fill in the blanks.

Mitten has white feet and black legs.

2. Mitten's feet are _____.

3. Mitten's legs are _____.

Fix the sentence.

4. little red riding hood had a basket

_____

WEEK 7 Tuesday

Circle the words that rhyme.

1. car   cat   hat

2. fish   fit   wish

Choose the best word. Write it on the line.

3. Lin will go _____ school.
              to   two

Fix the sentence.

4. when will fritz get here

_____

WEEK 7 **Wednesday**

Choose the best word. Write it on the line.

1. We _____ down the hill.
   slided   slid

2. I _____ my bike to the store.
   rided   rode

Read the sentence. Tell when it happened.

3. Tom made a snowman…

   in the summer. **OR** in the winter.

Fix the sentence.

4. order the pizza from pizza hut

_____

WEEK 7 **Thursday**

Circle the word that is spelled correctly.

1. pla   plai   play   pllaa

Fix the sentence.

2. *the little red hen* is a good bouk

_____

What happens next?

3. Jemma puts on her pajamas. Then…

   she goes outside to play. **OR** she hops into bed.

4. The clouds look black. Then…

   it starts to rain. **OR** my brother smiles.

WEEK 7 Friday

Finish each sentence two ways.

It could really happen.

The bird _____ .

Yesterday, the boy _____ .

It is make-believe.

The bird _____ .

Yesterday, the boy _____ .

WEEK 7 My Progress

How many did you get correct each day? Color the squares.

4				
3				
2				
1				
Monday	**Tuesday**	**Wednesday**	**Thursday**	**Friday**

WEEK 8 Monday

Is it a sentence?

1. Chocolate chip cookies.   yes   no

2. Peter fed the fish.   yes   no

3. Cookie Monster loves cookies.   yes   no

Fix the sentence.

4. they have baby goats at the wilson's farm

_____

_____

WEEK 8 Tuesday

Make two words in the -op family.

1. _____op   _____op

Write the opposite.

2. hard   _____

3. dark   _____

| light |
| soft |

Fix the sentence.

4. will you coom wth me to get ice cream

_____

WEEK 8 Wednesday

Circle the word that is spelled correctly.

1. stahp   stop   stp   stob

Choose the best word. Write it on the line.

2. Ms. Watson is a kindergarten teacher.

_____ has a colorful room.   (She   He)

3. Mr. Gorze loves books.

_____ always has one on his desk.   (She   He)

Fix the sentence.

4. peter pan lived in never-never land

_____

WEEK 8 Thursday

Circle the name that comes first in ABC order.

1. Bobby   Katie   Zander

2. Earl   Abdul   Mike

3. Sylvie   Nancy   Carmen

Fix the sentence.

4. next time, goldilocks will knock

_____

WEEK 8 Friday

Number the sentences in order to tell the story.
Then draw a picture that shows what happened next.

☐ Pedro asked his grandma if he could go.

☐ Tomas called Pedro on the phone.

☐ He asked him to come play.

WEEK 8 My Progress

How many did you get correct each day? Color the squares.

	Monday	Tuesday	Wednesday	Thursday	Friday
4					
3					
2					
1					

Monday

Make two words in the -it family.

1. _____ it   _____ it

Find the names. Fix the letters that should be capitals.

2. town   dallas

3. usa   country

Fix the sentence.

4. i want to go to disneyland

_____

Tuesday

Circle the words that rhyme with *fan*.

1. ran   sand   man   pan   can

Choose the best word. Write it on the line.

2. _____ want a cookie.
         me   I

3. Mr. Gerk and _____ worked together.
               me   I

Fix the sentence.

4. the box is from japan

_____

WEEK 9 Wednesday

Fix the sentence.

1. hannah and me went shopping

_____

Make a compound word.

2. side + walk = _____

3. class + room = _____

Answer the question.

4. Can a bird buy a car?   yes   no

WEEK 9 Thursday

Fix the sentence.

1. are we there yet

_____

Is it a question?

2. What color is the dog?   yes   no

3. How long will it take?   yes   no

4. I want to go home.   yes   no

WEEK 9 Friday

Write the words in the group where they belong.

Things in the Sky

_____

_____

_____

_____

Things on the Ground

_____

_____

_____

_____

Word Box

cloud   grass   house   bird   tree   tent   rainbow

WEEK 9 My Progress

How many did you get correct each day? Color the squares.

	Monday	Tuesday	Wednesday	Thursday	Friday
4					
3					
2					
1					

WEEK 10 Monday

Make two words in the -ad family.

1. _____ad _____ad

Write the word that means more than one.

2. one toy   three _____

3. one tree   two _____

Fix the sentence.

4. its a sunny dai

_____

WEEK 10 Tuesday

Write the two words for each contraction.

1. let's   _____ and _____

2. don't   _____ and _____

Circle the word that is spelled correctly.

3. git   gett   gt   get

Fix the sentence.

4. its cold at the north pole

_____

WEEK 10 Wednesday

Circle *real* or *make-believe*.

1. The mouse carried the groceries
   into the house.   real   make-believe

2. The mouse nibbled on the corn.   real   make-believe

3. The white mouse had pink eyes.   real   make-believe

Fix the sentence.

4. lets swim at the ymca

_____

WEEK 10 Thursday

Choose the best word. Write it on the line.

1. The girls _____ read the book.
              has   have

2. Carlos _____ a red coat.
           has   have

What happens next?

3. Noah puts milk on the cereal. Then...
   he gives it to his baby brother. **OR** he throws it in the trash.

Fix the sentence.

4. presidents' day is in february

_____

WEEK 10 Friday

Put the information into one sentence.

1. Chickens lay eggs.
   Turtles lay eggs.
   Stingrays lay eggs.

   _____

   _____

2. I can make a shadow.
   A tree can make a shadow.
   The moon can make a shadow.

   _____

   _____

Daily Language Review

WEEK 10 My Progress

How many did you get correct each day? Color the squares.

	Monday	Tuesday	Wednesday	Thursday	Friday
4					
3					
2					
1					

WEEK 11 Monday

Make two words in the -up family.

1. _____up   _____up

Circle the words that rhyme with *tent*.

2. bent   cent   ten   sent

3. went   tenth   rent   spent

Fix the sentence.

4. grandma is coming for passover

_____

WEEK 11 Tuesday

Choose the best word. Write it on the line.

1. _____ boys ran across the street.
   To   Two

2. I want a new book, _____.
   to   too

3. We went _____ the park.
   to   two

Fix the sentence.

4. we hide eggs for easter

_____

Wednesday

Choose the best word. Write it on the line.

1. Fred _____ his bat to school.

   brung   brought

2. Ellie _____ the ball over the fence.

   hitted   hit

Circle the word that is spelled correctly.

3. tha   thay   they   thye

Fix the sentence.

4. i can rid a bike

_____

Thursday

Fix the letters that should be capitals.

1. eric hill wrote the book *where's spot?*

2. at school, we read *where the wild things are.*

What might happen?

3. Tony was invited to a birthday party. So...

   he buys a present.   **OR**   he blows his nose.

Fix the sentence.

4. halloween is on friday

WEEK 11 Friday

This is Yoko. These are her things.
Use her name and 's to finish the labels.

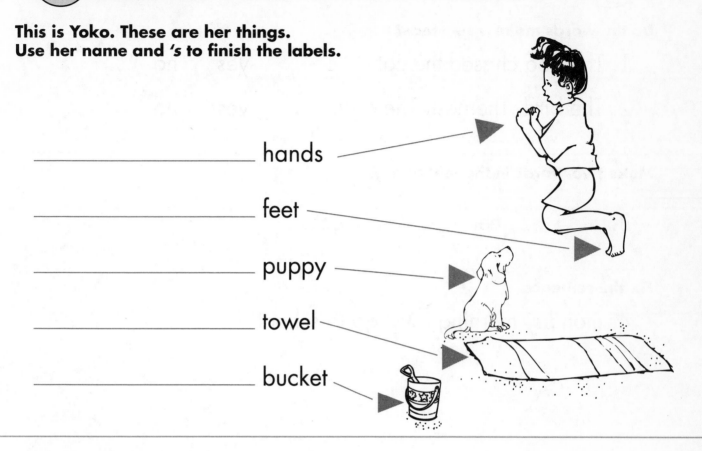

_____ hands

_____ feet

_____ puppy

_____ towel

_____ bucket

WEEK 11 My Progress

How many did you get correct each day? Color the squares.

	Monday	Tuesday	Wednesday	Thursday	Friday
4					
3					
2					
1					

WEEK 12 Monday

Do the words make a sentence?

1. The dog chased the cat.   yes   no

2. The bird. The nest. The egg.   yes   no

Make two words in the -eet family.

3. _____eet   _____eet

Fix the sentence.

4. monday morning i will go to school

_____

WEEK 12 Tuesday

Circle the word that is spelled correctly.

1. lok   luk   look   louk

Circle *real* or *make-believe*.

2. Sam rode the alligator to school.   real   make-believe

3. Sam rode the tractor to school.   real   make-believe

Fix the sentence.

4. *hop on pop* is a rhyming book

_____

© Evan-Moor Corp. • EMC 6821

WEEK 12 Wednesday

Read and decide.

1. Sally is wet. She is wearing a special suit. Is she...
   taking a bath? **OR** swimming?

2. Todd sniffed. Then he chewed his bone. Is Todd...
   a dog? **OR** a bird?

Write the opposite.

3. go _____

Fix the sentence.

4. i have a baby sister named penny

_____

WEEK 12 Thursday

Choose the best word. Write it on the line.

1. Mrs. Tripp likes to paint. _____ uses a big brush.
   Her   She

2. Mr. Jump likes to garden. _____ uses a little rake.
   He   Him

Write *first*, *next*, and *last* to tell the order.

3. _____   Baby had babies.

   _____   Baby was a puppy.

   _____   Baby grew up.

Fix the sentence.

4. do you have a vacation in july

_____

WEEK 12 Friday

Write the words in ABC order.

game   day   book   with   come

_____

_____

_____

_____

_____

WEEK 12 My Progress

How many did you get correct each day? Color the squares.

	Monday	Tuesday	Wednesday	Thursday	Friday
4					
3					
2					
1					

WEEK 13 Monday

Write your teacher's name.

1. _____

Read and decide.

2. If the paint spilled, there would be a mess.   true   false

3. If it rained, the ground would be dry.   true   false

Fix the sentence.

4. i called my story "the laughing cow"

_____

_____

WEEK 13 Tuesday

Circle *real* or *make-believe*.

1. The dog ate from a bowl.   real   make-believe

2. The dog drove a red car.   real   make-believe

Circle the word that is spelled correctly.

3. ball   boul   bol   bal

Fix the sentence.

4. december is a cold month

_____

Wednesday

Circle the words that rhyme with *dump*.

1. bump   dumb   grump   lump

Choose the best word. Write it on the line.

2. The table is big. Ten people can sit around _____.

   it   her

3. The mother cat is busy. _____ has four kittens.

   She   He

Fix the sentence.

4. what will you eat on thanksgiving

   _____

Thursday

Make a compound word.

1. sea + shell = _____

2. fire + fly = _____

Make two words in the *-ail* family.

3. _____ail   _____ail

Fix the sentence.

4. my brother is taller than steve

   _____

WEEK 13 Friday

Write the words in the group where they belong.

Tall Things   Short Things

_____   _____

_____   _____

_____   _____

Word Box

buildings   trees   ants   snails   giraffes   bushes

WEEK 13 My Progress

How many did you get correct each day? Color the squares.

	Monday	Tuesday	Wednesday	Thursday	Friday
4					
3					
2					
1					

WEEK 14 Monday

Make two words in the *-id* family.

1. _____id   _____id

Write the word that means more than one.

2. one mouse   two _____

3. one goose   two _____

Fix the sentence.

4. i celebrate kwanzaa

_____

WEEK 14 Tuesday

Write the two words for each contraction.

1. won't   _____ and _____

2. doesn't   _____ and _____

Circle the word that is spelled correctly.

3. make   mak   maak   maik

Fix the sentence.

4. did you decorate a tree for christmas

_____

WEEK 14 Wednesday

Read and decide.

1. The mouse yelled "Stop!" and ran away.   real   make-believe

2. The mouse squeaked and ran away.   real   make-believe

Write the answer on the line.

3. Mabel eats grass and hay. She doesn't like her saddle.

   Mabel is a _____. (cow   horse   pig)

Fix the sentence.

4. wednesday is in the middle of the week

   _____

WEEK 14 Thursday

Choose the best word. Write it on the line.

1. The boys _____ their favorite song.
   sing   sings

2. The girl _____ to the music.
   dance   dances

Fill in the blanks to complete the sentence.

3. A _____ is bigger than a _____.

Fix the sentence.

4. my dad reads the sunday paper

   _____

WEEK 14 Friday

Read the story. Then write what might happen next.

It was a warm day.
Trudy and Sammy were playing in the yard.
A big cloud blew in.
It covered the sun.

_____

_____

_____

Daily Language Review

WEEK 14 My Progress

How many did you get correct each day? Color the squares.

	Monday	Tuesday	Wednesday	Thursday	Friday
4					
3					
2					
1					

WEEK 15 **Monday**

Make two words in the *-ing* family.

1. _____ing   _____ing

Circle the capital letters.

2. P   d   F   f   L   k   R   A   q   C

Circle the words that rhyme with *crab*.

3. lab   crate   cab   tab

Fix the sentence.

4. last october i made a jack-o'-lantern

_____

WEEK 15 **Tuesday**

Circle the word that is spelled correctly.

1. fynd   find   feind   fid

2. tha   da   the   thea

Circle *real* or *make-believe*.

3. The elephant lost a shoe.   real   make-believe

   The horse lost a shoe.   real   make-believe

Fix the sentence.

4. soccer practice is on tuesday and thursday

_____

WEEK 15 Wednesday

Choose the best word. Write it on the line.

1. Mr. Brown read the book. _____ showed us the pictures, too.
   He   Him

2. Mrs. Roberts threw the ball. _____ made a basket.
   She   Her

Answer the question.

3. Is an elephant small?   yes   no

Fix the sentence.

4. tashas party is on friday

_____

WEEK 15 Thursday

Make a compound word.

1. butter + fly = _____

2. in + side = _____

3. air + plane = _____

Fix the sentence.

4. i filled the dogs bowl

_____

44

WEEK 15 Friday

Write the words in the group where they belong.

Living Things   Nonliving Things

_____   _____

_____   _____

_____   _____

Word Box

car   girl   tree   yo-yo   dog   bell

Daily Language Review

WEEK 15 My Progress

How many did you get correct each day? Color the squares.

	Monday	Tuesday	Wednesday	Thursday	Friday
4					
3					
2					
1					

WEEK 16 Monday

Make two words in the -ake family.

1. _____ake   _____ake

Circle the words that make a sentence.

2. We made cookies.   Good to eat.

3. Wagging its tail.   That puppy is cute.

Fix the sentence.

4. my dads car is blue

_____

WEEK 16 Tuesday

Circle the word that is spelled correctly.

1. grein   gren   green   grn

2. bloo   bleu   blu   blue

Circle real or make-believe.

3. The car zoomed down the road.   real   make-believe

Fix the sentence.

4. luke didnt want to go

_____

Daily Language Review

16 Wednesday

What happened next?

1. Tom lost his new mittens, so...

   he put on a hat. **OR** he wore an old pair.

2. The alarm went off, so...

   Dad got up. **OR** John put on his pajamas.

Write the opposite.

3. night _____

Fix the sentence.

4. kennys coat is missing

_____

Daily Language Review

16 Thursday

Choose the best word. Write it on the line.

1. Sally and Tom ran home. _____ wanted a snack.
   They   Them

2. The cars waited. When the light changed, _____ left.
   they   them

Circle which came first.

3. Rick baked the cake.   Rick sang "Happy Birthday."

Fix the sentence.

4. wont you come with me

_____

© Evan-Moor Corp. • EMC 6821

47

WEEK 16 Friday

Mrs. Kehl's class has to go to lunch in **ABC** order.
Make a list to help the students line up in order.

David   Andy   Chase   Heather

Barbie   Evan   Felice   Grant

1. _____   5. _____

2. _____   6. _____

3. _____   7. _____

4. _____   8. _____

WEEK 16 My Progress

How many did you get correct each day? Color the squares.

	Monday	Tuesday	Wednesday	Thursday	Friday
4					
3					
2					
1					

WEEK 17 Monday

Make two words in the -ent family.

1. _____ent   _____ent

Fix the words that need capital letters.

2. bambi   horse   mickey mouse   boy

3. home   washington   united states   farm

Fix the sentence.

4. miss browns key is on the table

_____

WEEK 17 Tuesday

Circle the words that rhyme with boy.

1. toy   bow   Roy   joy

Circle the word that is spelled correctly.

2. lik   like   lyke   lic

3. thes   thez   this   thisth

Fix the sentence.

4. tommy wants to see michael jordan

_____

WEEK 17 Wednesday

Circle *real* or *make-believe*.

1. The letter is in the mailbox.   real   make-believe

2. The lady is in the mailbox.   real   make-believe

Choose the best words. Write them on the line.

3. _____ can go to the park.
   Me and you   You and I

Fix the sentence.

4. please hand me sharlas book

_____

WEEK 17 Thursday

Choose the best word. Write it on the line.

1. Ms. White _____ my paper.
   taked   took

2. I _____ a robin.
   saw   seen

Write two words for the contraction.

3. isn't _____ and _____

Fix the sentence.

4. i and my dad mowed the lawn

WEEK 17 Friday

Write a sentence to answer each question. Then write your own question.

1. What do you like to eat?

   _____

2. What is your favorite color?

   _____

3. What will you do this weekend?

   _____

4. Write your own question.

   _____

WEEK 17 My Progress

How many did you get correct each day? Color the squares.

	Monday	Tuesday	Wednesday	Thursday	Friday
4					
3					
2					
1					

WEEK 18 Monday

Choose the best word. Write it on the line.

1. Bill and Sue _____ on the playground.

   were   was

2. They used to _____ playing on the bars.

   like   liked

Make two words in the -ub family.

3. _____ub   _____ub

Fix the sentence.

4. tom gots a new toy car

_____

WEEK 18 Tuesday

Write the word that means more than one.

1. one bird   three _____

2. one man   two _____

Circle real or make-believe.

3. The airplane flew in the sky.   real   make-believe

Fix the sentence.

4. the mail isnt here yet

_____

WEEK 18 Wednesday

Write two words for each contraction.

1. I'll _____ and _____

2. that's _____ and _____

What will happen?

3. Tomorrow is my birthday, so...

   I will have a party. **OR** I'll go to the dentist.

Fix the sentence.

4. mrs brown called on jose

_____

WEEK 18 Thursday

Circle the word that is spelled correctly.

1. haf   hav   have   haav

2. girl   gerl   grl   gil

What does it mean? Draw to show.

3. Todd used the bar of soap.

Fix the sentence.

4. ill bring it to you

_____

WEEK 18 Friday

Read and decide. Then write the answer.

The little bird flew up.
The little bird flew down.
The little bird looked for a good place.

The little bird has some string.
The little bird has some straw.
What is the little bird doing?

_____

_____

Daily Language Review

WEEK 18 My Progress

How many did you get correct each day? Color the squares.

	Monday	Tuesday	Wednesday	Thursday	Friday
4					
3					
2					
1					

WEEK 19 Monday

Make two words in the -ay family.

1. _____ay _____ay

Choose the best word. Write it on the line.

2. I went to _____ house.
there   their

3. Put the pencil over _____.
there   their

Fix the sentence.

4. thats a good book

_____

WEEK 19 Tuesday

Circle the words that rhyme.

1. will   Bill   doll   fill

2. him   bit   kit   hit

What happens next?

3. Mama cuts the apple into little bits. Then...

she makes a pie.   **OR**   she goes for a walk.

Fix the sentence.

4. will you please call donna for me

_____

WEEK 19 Wednesday

Whose is it? Write the answer on the line.

Cari's <u>toy bunny</u> and Todd's <u>toy puppy</u> sat on the table.
        1   **2**

1. _____   2. _____

Choose the best word. Write it on the line.

3. He _____ a cookie.
            take   took

Fix the sentence.

4. me and my buddy play together

_____

WEEK 19 Thursday

Circle the word that is spelled correctly.

1. duz   dus   does   doos

2. will   wil   wel   weel

Circle _real_ or _make-believe_.

3. The tow truck pulled the mountain.   real   make-believe

Fix the sentence.

4. come with i to see the birds

_____

WEEK 19 Friday

Read the address on the envelope. Fix the words that need capital letters.

mr. peter rabbit

2 mulberry lane

sussex, england

WEEK 19 My Progress

How many did you get correct each day? Color the squares.

	Monday	Tuesday	Wednesday	Thursday	Friday
4					
3					
2					
1					

WEEK 20 Monday

Make two words in the -ook family.

1. _____ook   _____ook

Circle the words that make a sentence.

2. Tommy lives in town.   In a very big house.

3. The best basketball player.   Kareem is on the team.

Fix the sentence.

4. me and my friends went to see *bambi*

_____

WEEK 20 Tuesday

Circle the word that is spelled correctly.

1. tym   teim   time   tiem

2. tuday   todai   tooday   today

Circle *real* or *make-believe*.

3. The sky is falling.   real   make-believe

Fix the sentence.

4. nick and carmen isn't home yet

_____

© Evan-Moor Corp. • EMC 6821

WEEK 20 Wednesday

What will happen?

1. The little arrow is pointing to the **E**, so...

    Dad puts gas in the car. **OR** we stop for an elephant.

2. I like to read *Stellaluna* over and over, so...

    I hug my dog. **OR** I check it out of the library.

Write the opposite.

3. come _____

Fix the sentence.

4. he sung a good song

_____

WEEK 20 Thursday

Circle the name that comes first in ABC order.

1. Mandy   Sarah   Kayli

2. Sven   Abe   Nick

Choose the best words. Write them on the line.

3. _____ will be late for school.
   Me and you   You and I

Fix the sentence.

4. the team wore there red hats

_____

WEEK 20 Friday

Number the pictures in order. Then write about what happened.

_____

_____

_____

WEEK 20 My Progress

How many did you get correct each day? Color the squares.

	Monday	Tuesday	Wednesday	Thursday	Friday
4					
3					
2					
1					

WEEK 21 Monday

Make two words in the -ug family.

1. _____ug   _____ug

Fix the words that need capital letters.

2. mrs.   mr.   ms.   o'clock   dr.

3. the   tom   them   tyler   to

Fix the sentence.

4. us want a bag of popcorn

_____

WEEK 21 Tuesday

Name:

Circle the word that is spelled correctly.

1. abut   abot   abowt   about

2. frum   from   frm   frahm

Circle real or make-believe.

3. The Big Bad Wolf blew down the pig's house.
   real   make-believe

Fix the sentence.

4. i can do it more better

_____

WEEK 21 Wednesday

Choose the best word. Write it on the line.

1. Ms. White blows _____ whistle when it's time to line up.
   her   his

2. Mr. Vaas rides _____ bike to school.
   her   his

Circle the word that does <u>not</u> belong.

3. shoes   gloves   socks   boots

Fix the sentence.

4. i gots a letter frm granny

_____

WEEK 21 Thursday   Name:

Make a compound word.

1. some + thing = _____

2. note + book = _____

Choose the best word. Write it on the line.

3. I don't have _____ money.
   no   any

Fix the sentence.

4. will pat come to beths party

_____

WEEK 21 Friday

Sophia is a new girl at your school. Write three questions that you would like to ask her.

_____

_____

_____

_____

_____

_____

WEEK 21 My Progress

How many did you get correct each day? Color the squares.

	Monday	Tuesday	Wednesday	Thursday	Friday
4					
3					
2					
1					

WEEK 22 Monday

Make two words in the -ip family.

1. _____ip   _____ip

Circle the word that means more than one.

2. man   men

3. people   person

Fix the sentence.

4. the girls has read the story about harry

_____

WEEK 22 Tuesday

Write the contraction.

1. you will = _____

2. you have = _____

Circle real or make-believe.

3. The bear stood on its hind legs.   real   make-believe

Fix the sentence.

4. he play ball after school yesterday

_____

WEEK 22 Wednesday

Circle the word that is spelled correctly.

1. schul   schol   skool   school

2. went   wint   whent   wnt

What happens next?

3. Mom gives Elise a quarter for helping with the wash. Then...

Elise buries the quarter in the backyard.

OR

Elise puts the quarter in her bank.

Fix the sentence.

4. youll need a hatt and mittens

_____

WEEK 22 Thursday

Choose the best word. Write it on the line.

1. They _____ all going to Tina's house.
     was   were

2. Monty _____ staying home.
     was   were

3. He's the _____ dad.
     best   bestest

Fix the sentence.

4. can you help the new grl wth hir buks

_____

WEEK 22 Friday

Read the clue. Write a number to tell which house the child lives in.

1.    2.    3.

☐ Brett loves to hear the water splash outside his window.

☐ Susie doesn't have to go outside to visit her neighbors.

☐ Ann and the third little pig in the story live in the same kind of house.

WEEK 22 My Progress

How many did you get correct each day? Color the squares.

	Monday	Tuesday	Wednesday	Thursday	Friday
4					
3					
2					
1					

WEEK 23 **Monday**

Make two words in the *-and* family.

1. _____ and _____ and

Choose the best word. Write it on the line.

2. Karen had _____ cookies.

four   for

3. She made them _____ Dennis.

four   for

Fix the sentence.

4. youre my bestest friend

_____

WEEK 23 **Tuesday**

Circle the words that rhyme.

1. ball   bell   wall

2. room   zoo   zoom

Circle the word that is spelled correctly.

3. hus   house   hows   howse

Fix the sentence.

4. please tell i all abowt your gaim

_____

WEEK 23 Wednesday

Finish the sentences to answer the questions.

1. Whose bowl is it?   It is the _____.

2. Whose cat is it?   It is the _____.

3. Whose collar is it?   It is the _____.

Fix the sentence.

4. josie and i cant buy no candy

_____

WEEK 23 Thursday

Choose the best word. Write it on the line.

1. I _____ a happy boy.

   drawed   drew

2. Sammy _____ fast.

   runned   ran

Circle the word that is spelled correctly.

3. doun   dwn   down   dahwn

Fix the sentence.

4. we hav went to the park every saturday

WEEK 23 Friday

Fix the note.

dear miss muffet

im afraid of spiders two was yr mom mad
that you spilled yr curds and whey i hope not

yr friend

andy

WEEK 23 My Progress

How many did you get correct each day? Color the squares.

	Monday	Tuesday	Wednesday	Thursday	Friday
4					
3					
2					
1					

WEEK 24 Monday

Circle the words that make a sentence.

1. The leaves are falling.   Red, yellow, and brown.

2. Baking a batch of cookies.   Mom is busy.

Make two words in the -ig family.

3. _____ig   _____ig

Fix the sentence.

4. i runned faster than stevie and pete

_____

WEEK 24 Tuesday

Circle the word that is spelled correctly.

1. wahnt   wnt   want   waant

2. sed   sayd   sayed   said

Circle real or make-believe.

3. The fish swam in a school.   real   make-believe

Fix the sentence.

4. wll you fynd the bawl i lost

_____

WEEK 24 Wednesday

What is happening?

1. Mom pins the pattern to the cloth. She cuts it out and sews it.
   Mom is making a dress. **OR** Mom is cleaning the house.

2. Bubba writes a note. He folds it up. He puts it in an envelope.
   Bubba is doing homework. **OR** Bubba is sending a letter.

Write the opposite.

3. short _____

Fix the sentence.

4. i rided my bike to marys house

_____

WEEK 24 Thursday

Choose the best word. Write it on the line.

1. My brother and _____ will help do it.
   me   I

2. _____ didn't have time.
   They   Them

Circle the word that comes first in ABC order.

3. dog   rat   mouse   bird   tiger

Fix the sentence.

4. my lttl sistr cant never tie hr shoes

_____

WEEK 24 Friday

Write numbers to show the order of the sentences to tell a story.

☐ They went home happy.

☐ One day, Little Bear went for a walk.

☐ They found some honey and ate it.

☐ He met one of his friends.

WEEK 24 My Progress

How many did you get correct each day? Color the squares.

	Monday	Tuesday	Wednesday	Thursday	Friday
4					
3					
2					
1					

WEEK 25 **Monday**

Make two words in the -en family.

1. _____en   _____en

Circle the word that is spelled correctly.

2. when   whin   whean   whn

3. suum   some   somme   sme

Fix the sentence.

4. he dont like tomatoes

_____

WEEK 25 **Tuesday**

Circle the words that rhyme.

1. cake   cook   bake   back

2. sun   sing   sink   wing

Circle real or make-believe.

3. The duck quacked and swam away.   real   make-believe

Fix the sentence.

4. peter dont wnt to plai wth me

_____

WEEK 25 Wednesday

Choose the best word. Write it on the line.

1. Mr. Peters likes to fish. _____ always catches something.

He   Him

2. Can you read the names? _____ are hard to see.

They   Them

Circle the word that does <u>not</u> belong.

3. tractor   barn   skyscraper   haystack

Fix the sentence.

4. du you lke mi gren dress

_____

WEEK 25 Thursday   Name:

Make a compound word.

1. pan + cake = _____

2. base + ball = _____

Circle the question.

3. May I have some milk?   Two cookies with frosting?

Fix the sentence.

4. my mom wont leave me do it

_____

WEEK 25 Friday

Fix the list.

Things to Remember

tommys bike tire

pizza from pizza hut

wrapping papr

monopoly gme

WEEK 25 My Progress

How many did you get correct each day? Color the squares.

	Monday	Tuesday	Wednesday	Thursday	Friday
4					
3					
2					
1					

Monday

Write the word that means more than one.

1. one box   three _____

2. one lady   two _____

Make two words in the -og family.

3. _____og   _____og

Fix the sentence.

4. i dont have no money

_____

Daily Language Review

WEEK 26 **Tuesday**

Write the contraction.

1. has + not = _____

2. have + not = _____

Circle the word that is spelled correctly.

3. yer   yor   your   yr

Fix the sentence.

4. tony the tiger lks frosted flakes

_____

WEEK 26 Wednesday

Choose the best word. Write it on the line.

1. James _____ to ride the bus home.
   have   has

2. Doug and Colby _____ a computer at home.
   have   has

What will happen next?

3. Joe turns on the television. Then...

   he runs outside to play.   **OR**   he sits down to watch.

Fix the sentence.

4. pedro hasnt misst one dai

_____

WEEK 26 Thursday

Choose the best word. Write it on the line.

1. A snail is _____ than a ladybug.
   bigger   biggest

2. My pillow is the _____ thing in my room.
   softer   softest

Could it be true?

3. The hamster lives in a cage.   yes   no

Fix the sentence.

4. fred brung his bat to schul

_____

WEEK 26 Friday

Circle the things you need to bake a cake.

bowl   flour   tennis shoes   eggs

catcher's mitt   sugar   spoon   oven

cake pan   rake   recipe   mittens

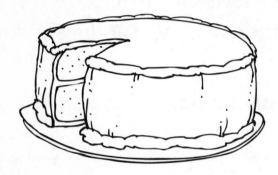

WEEK 26 My Progress

How many did you get correct each day? Color the squares.

	Monday	Tuesday	Wednesday	Thursday	Friday
4					
3					
2					
1					

WEEK 27 Monday

Make two words in the -am family.

1. _____ am   _____ am

Choose the best word. Write it on the line.

2. Sammy _____ the book.
red   read

3. The strawberries are bright _____.
red   read

Fix the sentence.

4. my mom don't allow no tv after dinner.

_____

WEEK 27 Tuesday

Circle the words that rhyme.

1. log   frog   lion   hog

2. sand   hand   fan   band

Choose the best word. Write it on the line.

3. Tom likes to _____ the ball at recess.
kick   kicked

Fix the sentence.

4. its fun to ply at schul

_____

WEEK 27 Wednesday

Write who it belongs to.

Mr. Black lives in a purple house. Mr. Brown lives in a white house.

1. Whose house is white?   Mr. _____

2. Whose house is purple?   Mr. _____

Circle real or make-believe.

3. When the princess kissed the frog, he turned into a prince.

real   make-believe

Fix the sentence.

4. we slided down the hill

_____

WEEK 27 Thursday

Circle the word that is spelled correctly.

1. muther   moher   mather   mother

2. white   wheyet   wite   yiite

What is happening?

3. Mom squeezes the lemons and adds sugar. Then she pours in water and stirs. Mom is...

making lemonade.   **OR**   fixing a salad.

Fix the sentence.

4. dad founded moms letter on the table

_____

WEEK 27 Friday

Betty wrote this poem for her mother. Fix the underlined words.

Roses are <u>read</u>.

<u>violets</u> are blue.

<u>im</u> glad that I have

A mom <u>lick</u> you.

1. _____

2. _____

3. _____

4. _____

WEEK 27 My Progress

How many did you get correct each day? Color the squares.

	Monday	Tuesday	Wednesday	Thursday	Friday
4					
3					
2					
1					

WEEK 28 Monday

Circle the word that is spelled correctly.

1. cuud   cood   could   cude

2. fahther   fathur   father   fother

Make two words in the -ice family.

3. _____ice   _____ice

Fix the sentence.

4. i have red yellow and blue paint

_____

WEEK 28 Tuesday

Circle the words that make a sentence.

1. The little bird built a nest.   Standing on the branch.

2. Two little blue eggs.   The bird chirped happily.

Circle real or make-believe.

3. The cat climbed the tree, trying to catch the bird.
         real   make-believe

Fix the sentence.

4. whin wil you go two seans house

_____

WEEK 28 Wednesday

What will you need?

1. For the baseball game:

   glove   hat   sled   skates   ball

2. For the bike ride:

   helmet   yo-yo   water bottle   bike   pump

Write the opposite.

3. black   _____

Fix the sentence.

4. mrs tang made cookies cake and pie.

   _____

WEEK 28 Thursday

Choose the best word. Write it on the line.

1. _____ dogs bark all the time.
   Them   Those

2. I want some of _____ cookies.
   them   those

Circle the word that comes first in ABC order.

3. red   blue   pink   yellow

Fix the sentence.

4. we took food water and a tent

   _____

WEEK 28 Friday

Find all the words that tell *where*. Circle them.

The funny clown ran around the car.

First, he got in it.

Then, he got out.

He crawled over the car.

He even crawled under it.

Where could he be now?

WEEK 28 My Progress

How many did you get correct each day? Color the squares.

	Monday	Tuesday	Wednesday	Thursday	Friday
4					
3					
2					
1					

WEEK 29 Monday

Make two words in the -aw family.

1. _____aw   _____aw

Circle the word that is spelled correctly.

2. lettle   litle   little   littl

3. whre   whare   wahre   where

Fix the sentence.

4. Abdul wont fnd nothing in the box

_____

WEEK 29 Tuesday

Fix the words that need capital letters.

1. sari, ann, and i went home.

2. bree, todd, and whitney rode to central park.

Circle the words that rhyme.

3. pen   hen   tan   ten   pin   men

Fix the sentence.

4. ann hided under the bed

_____

WEEK 29 Wednesday

Circle *real* or *make-believe*.

1. The men talked to the boys.   real   make-believe

2. The hen talked to the boys.   real   make-believe

Choose the best word. Write it on the line.

3. _____ read a book last night.

    I   Me

Fix the sentence.

4. shes the most tall in our class

_____

WEEK 29 Thursday

Make a compound word.

1. cake + walk = _____

2. play + ground = _____

Unscramble the words to make a question. Add end punctuation.

3. old How you are

_____

Fix the sentence.

4. pauls more faster than i am

_____

WEEK 29 Friday

Some words sound alike, but they mean different things and have different spellings. Draw pictures to show what the two same-sound words mean.

Tom's plate is **bare**.	The **bear** had a cub.

WEEK 29 My Progress

How many did you get correct each day? Color the squares.

	Monday	Tuesday	Wednesday	Thursday	Friday
4					
3					
2					
1					

WEEK 30 Monday

Write the contraction.

1. would + not = _____

2. could + not = _____

Make two words in the -ive family.

3. _____ive   _____ive

Fix the sentence.

4. tha grl lived in tha gren huse

_____

WEEK 30 Tuesday

Circle the words that mean more than one.

1. hog   chickens   kitten   cattle

2. men   girl   boys   woman

Circle real or make-believe.

3. The paint dripped on the floor.   real   make-believe

Fix the sentence.

4. my litle sistr hitted the ball hard

_____

WEEK 30 Wednesday

Circle the word that is spelled correctly.

1. thenk   thinck   thnk   think
2. bahk   back   bck   baack

What happens next?

3. Ben puts the kernels in the pot and plugs it in. Then he...

   hears the baby cry.   **OR**   hears popping sounds.

Fix the sentence.

4. i aint gonna do that

_____

WEEK 30 Thursday

Choose the best word. Write it on the line.

1. Cherie _____ like peanut butter.
   doesn't   don't

2. The boys _____ like pea soup.
   doesn't   don't

Finish the word.

3. Your foot is long____ than the baby's foot.

Fix the sentence.

4. my dog spot growed bigger

_____

WEEK 30 Friday

Andy wrote this note to Sam. Can you fix it?

sam,

    meet me at the park

on south street i hav sumthing

special to show yu

    andy

Daily Language Review

WEEK 30 My Progress

How many did you get correct each day? Color the squares.

	Monday	Tuesday	Wednesday	Thursday	Friday
4					
3					
2					
1					

WEEK 31 Monday

Circle the words that rhyme.

1. big   bug   rub   rug

Add the commas.

2. Sunday May 1 2010

Make two words in the -et family.

3. _____et   _____et

Fix the sentence.

4. wll you call mrs groom for me

_____

WEEK 31 Tuesday

Choose the best word. Write it on the line.

1. Chad walked _____ the library.

to   too

2. Billy's little brother wanted to come, _____.

two   too

What happens next?

3. Mom puts sandwiches and fruit in a basket. She says we are ... going to have a picnic. **OR** going to clean the house.

Fix the sentence.

4. whre do you live

_____

WEEK 31 Wednesday

Choose the best word. Write it on the line.

1. Yesterday, I _____ to the zoo.
went   goed

2. We _____ our bikes home.
rided   rode

Finish the word.

3. Tom_____ shoe came untied.

Fix the sentence.

4. i lickt tha buk abowt tha duck named ping

_____

WEEK 31 Thursday

Circle the word that is spelled correctly.

1. sah   saw   sahw   cah

2. oaver   ofer   ovr   over

Circle real or make-believe.

3. The dragon breathed fire and smoke.   real   make-believe

Fix the sentence.

4. dr seuss liked to write funny buks

_____

WEEK 31 Friday

Write the words in the group where they belong.

Soft Things   Hard Things

_____   _____

_____   _____

_____   _____

Word Box

| pillow | rock | sidewalk | T-shirt | marble | fur |

WEEK 31 My Progress

How many did you get correct each day? Color the squares.

	Monday	Tuesday	Wednesday	Thursday	Friday
4					
3					
2					
1					

WEEK 32 Monday

Circle the word that is spelled correctly.

1. hme   hoam   hom   home

2. tok   took   touk   tuk

Make two words in the -ick family.

3. _____ick   _____ick

Fix the sentence.

4. me and chichi wants to plai at donnys house

_____

WEEK 32 Tuesday

Circle the words that make a sentence.

1. Milly and the cute puppy.   He's so soft.

2. The water spilled.   Too many puddles in the yard.

Circle real or make-believe.

3. When she sprinkled magic dust on the pumpkin, it turned into a carriage.

real   make-believe

Fix the sentence.

4. cinderella weared a beautiful dress two the kings ball

_____

WEEK 32 Wednesday

Write the opposite.

1. front   _____

2. to   _____

Read and decide.

3. Camille put on her new dress and brushed her hair. Her dad had promised to take her...

     to a concert.   **OR**   on a hike.

Fix the sentence.

4. which shoes should i wear to saturdays gaim

_____

WEEK 32 Thursday

Choose the best word. Write it on the line.

1. _____ wants to come with us.
     Her   She

2. I don't think Mother will let _____ come.
                            her   she

Circle the word that comes first in ABC order.

3. Pluto   Donald   Mickey   Goofy

Fix the sentence.

4. i didnt see no mickey mouse at disneyland

WEEK 32 Friday

Write 1, 2, and 3 under the pictures to tell the order.

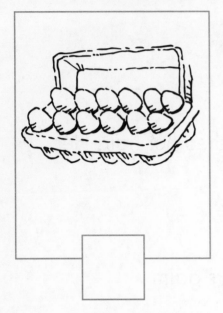

WEEK 32 My Progress

How many did you get correct each day? Color the squares.

	Monday	Tuesday	Wednesday	Thursday	Friday
4					
3					
2					
1					

WEEK 33 Monday

Choose the best word. Write it on the line.

1. _____ can't reach the book.
   He   Him

2. Will you please help _____?
   he   him

Make two words in the -ap family.

3. _____ap   _____ap

Fix the sentence.

4. ron was afraid of bruces dog

_____

WEEK 33 Tuesday

Fix the words that should be capitals.

1. mr. felix smith
   301 glenmere blvd.
   evans, colorado

Circle the words that rhyme.

2. cake   cup   bake   rake

Add the commas.

3. August 31 2010

Fix the sentence.

4. ms green wnts all the girls to taik tomorrows test

WEEK 33 **Wednesday**

Circle the word that is spelled correctly.

1. peeple   peaple   peopl   people

2. storee   stoary   story   storie

Circle _real_ or _make-believe_.

3. The swimming pool was filled with lemonade.

            real   make-believe

Fix the sentence.

4. i need a hat a ball and mi bat

_____

WEEK 33 **Thursday**

Choose the best word. Write it on the line.

1. _____ dogs run fast.
    Them   Those

2. He broke _____ eggs.
           them   those

Make a compound word.

3. mail + box = _____

Fix the sentence.

4. can patty and grace com over to spend the nite

WEEK 33 Friday

Write the words in the group where they belong.

Real People	Make-Believe Characters
_____	_____
_____	_____
_____	_____
_____	_____

Word Box

Peter Pan	Abraham Lincoln	Christopher Columbus	Superman
Dr. Seuss	Big Bad Wolf	Martin Luther King, Jr.	Pinocchio

WEEK 33 My Progress

How many did you get correct each day? Color the squares.

4					
3					
2					
1					
	Monday	Tuesday	Wednesday	Thursday	Friday

Choose the best word. Write it on the line.

1. The boys _____ the balls at the target.
   throw   throws

2. The girls _____ up the steep steps.
   climb   climbs

Fix the sentence.

3. tina and tasha rided to burger king

_____

What happens next?

4. Scott puts on his pjs and brushes his teeth. Then he...
   goes out for a walk.   **OR**   jumps into bed.

Write the contraction.

1. that + is = _____

2. he + is = _____

Make two words in the -unk family.

3. _____unk   _____unk

Fix the sentence.

4. i will use dads paintbrush two paint the wall

_____

WEEK 34 Wednesday

Choose the best word. Write it on the line.

1. There were three _____ in the cage.
   mouses   mice

2. The _____ flew in a giant V.
   gooses   geese

Circle real or make-believe.

3. The man balanced on the tightrope
   and walked across without falling.   real   make-believe

Fix the sentence.

4. toby and me are going to the big top circus

_____

WEEK 34 Thursday

Circle the word that is spelled correctly.

1. weer   wher   were   wer

2. jist   just   jst   jahst

Choose the best word. Write it on the line.

3. Franco has the _____ chair in our classroom.
   bigger   biggest

Fix the sentence.

4. have you red the buk about peter rabbit

_____

WEEK 34 Friday

Read and decide. Then write the answer.

I have a surprise in my hand.
It is small and white.
It has a long tail and whiskers.
Its name starts with an **m**.
What could it be?

_____

WEEK 34 My Progress

How many did you get correct each day? Color the squares.

	Monday	Tuesday	Wednesday	Thursday	Friday
4					
3					
2					
1					

WEEK 35 Monday

Choose the best word. Write it on the line.

1. I _____ the answer to that question.

   know   no

2. There are _____ more apples on the tree.

   know   no

Make two words in the -ool family.

3. _____ool   _____ool

Fix the sentence.

4. next year, im not gonna go to no picnics

_____

WEEK 35 Tuesday

Choose the best word. Write it on the line.

1. Coach _____ me how to kick the ball.

   learned   taught

2. The boys _____ a mess with the paints.

   maked   made

Circle the word that is spelled correctly.

3. woo   who   wu   whoou

Fix the sentence.

4. alice and me isnt going over their

_____

WEEK 35 Wednesday

Write who it belongs to.

Lindy has a blue bike. Jean has a red bike.

1. _____ bike is red.

2. _____ bike is blue.

Read and decide.

3. Ms. Rupp put on her boots, her coat, and her umbrella. Is it... sunny? **OR** stormy?

Fix the sentence.

4. she dont want to stawp at tims house

_____

WEEK 35 Thursday

Circle *real* or *make-believe*.

1. Tommy climbed up the tree and waved to me.

real   make-believe

2. The turtle climbed up the tree and waved to me.

real   make-believe

Circle the words that rhyme.

3. claw   clap   straw   crawl   draw

Fix the sentence.

4. next july, im moving to california

WEEK 35 Friday

Fix the note.

june 30 2010

dear grandpa

　　　thank you for the new

bukits my favorite kind

i cant wait to read it

i love you

　　　　　frank

WEEK 35 My Progress

How many did you get correct each day? Color the squares.

	Monday	Tuesday	Wednesday	Thursday	Friday
4					
3					
2					
1					

WEEK 36 Monday

Circle the questions.

1. Can Sally come over?   Come soon?

2. Stop and go now?   Will Henry stop here?

Make two words in the *-old* family.

3. _____old   _____old

Fix the sentence.

4. kelly touk the buk to lilys sister

_____

WEEK 36 Tuesday

Circle the word that is spelled correctly.

1. vehry   viry   vry   very

2. smahl   smoll   small   smll

Circle *real* or *make-believe*.

3. The wolf blew down the house.   real   make-believe

Fix the sentence.

4. we runned around the block for times

_____

WEEK 36 Wednesday

What will happen?

1. Riley poured the hot tea over the ice cubes.

_____

2. Rosa mixed the yellow and the blue paint.

_____

Write the opposite.

3. under _____

Fix the sentence.

4. will you learn me how to swim on monday

_____

WEEK 36 Thursday

Choose the best word. Write it on the line.

1. Colby and _____ went to the movie.

    I   me

2. Mr. Graham gave the paper to _____ .

    I   me

Circle the word that comes first in ABC order.

3. oranges   lemons   pineapple   grapefruit

Fix the sentence.

4. hes going to jims house

_____

WEEK 36 Friday

Number the sentences in order.

☐ The rain stopped and a rainbow appeared.

☐ The clouds got dark and it started to rain.

☐ The flowers smiled in the sunshine after their bath.

☐ Brenda enjoyed a wet walk under her umbrella.

WEEK 36 My Progress

How many did you get correct each day? Color the squares.

	Monday	Tuesday	Wednesday	Thursday	Friday
4					
3					
2					
1					

Good for You

You have successfully completed

Daily Language Review

Sentence Editing Checklist

Use this checklist to help correct the daily sentence.

 Does each sentence begin with a capital letter?

 Does each sentence end with a period, a question mark, or an exclamation point?

 Do names of people, places, and other proper nouns, such as books, songs, and poems, begin with a capital letter?

 Did I use a period in abbreviations and initials?

 Did I use apostrophes to show possession (Anna's desk) and in contractions (isn't)?

 Did I choose the correct word?
- homophones (to, two, too)
- verbs (is, are)
- pronouns (he, him)

 Did I check for spelling errors?

 Did I place commas where they are needed?
words in a series
addresses, dates
dialogue
compound sentences
introductory phrases

 Did I underline the names of books, magazines, movies, and plays?

 Did I use quotation marks
to show the exact words being spoken?
around the names of poems, songs, and short stories?